A Christian Perspective
on the Hebrew Israelites

By

Carlton Green

A Christian Perspective
on the Hebrew Israelites

Unless otherwise indicated, all scriptures are quoted from
the King James Version of the Bible.

Published by: To His Glory Publishing Company, Inc.
(770) 458-7947
www.tohisglorypublishing.com

This Book is available at:
Amazon.com, BarnesandNoble.com, Booksamillion.com,
UK, EU, Canada, Australia, etc.

Also call or email below to order this book.
(770) 458-7947
Email: tohisglorypublishing@yahoo.com

ISBN: 978-1-942724-10-0

Introduction

How this Book Came About

This book is the result of a conversation that I had with a **Hebrew Israelite** (a non-Jewish religious sect) that lasted all day; **11am – 7:30pm**! After that conversation, my heart was heavy because their explanations of placing the Old Testament before the New Testament was an eye opener for me. Meaning, their contrary belief of **placing faith only in the Old Testament**. Since that conversation, I have learned that there are many belief systems in the Hebrew Israelite Camp; just like there are many denominations in the Christian Church. **For instance, there are Hebrew Israelites who teach that Salvation is obtained by keeping 'The Law' also known to many as the Law of Moses. This belief includes keeping the Sabbath Day and observing the Feast Days outlined in Leviticus 23.** For those not familiar with these Feasts, they are in **Leviticus 23:4-42** and here are some of them:

> "4 These are the feasts of the LORD, even holy convocations, which ye shall proclaim in their seasons. 5 In the fourteenth day of the first month at even is the **LORD'S passover.** 6 And on the fifteenth day of the same month is **the feast of unleavened bread unto the LORD:** seven days ye must eat unleavened bread…24 Speak unto the children of Israel, saying, In the seventh month, in the first day of the month, shall ye have a sabbath, **a memorial of blowing of trumpets, an holy convocation…** 27Also on the tenth day of this seventh month there shall be **a day of atonement: it shall be an holy convocation unto you; and ye shall**

afflict your souls, and offer an offering made by fire unto the LORD...

37 **These are the feasts of the LORD, which ye shall proclaim to be holy convocations, to offer an offering made by fire unto the LORD, a burnt offering, and a meat offering, a sacrifice, and drink offerings, everything upon his day:** 38 Beside the sabbaths of the LORD, and beside your gifts, and beside all your vows, and beside all your freewill offerings, which ye give unto the LORD. 39 Also in the fifteenth day of the seventh month, **when ye have gathered in the fruit of the land, ye shall keep a feast unto the LORD seven days:** on the first day shall be a sabbath, and on the eighth day shall be a sabbath.

40 And ye shall take you on the first day the boughs of goodly trees, branches of palm trees, and the boughs of thick trees, and willows of the brook; and ye shall rejoice before the LORD your God seven days. 41 **And ye shall keep it a feast unto the LORD seven days in the year.** It shall be a statute forever in your generations: ye shall celebrate it in the seventh month. 42 **Ye shall dwell in booths seven days;** all that are Israelites born shall dwell in booths..."

<u>**This book is not dealing with the subject of who the real Hebrew Israelites are (Jews),**</u> **because only God knows who they are. This book is dealing with correcting the erroneous teaching of a Salvation by Works** because, the true biblical teaching is that Salvation is only obtained in Jesus Christ and by faith in Him alone. It is only by grace and nothing else.

Therefore, to teach anything else is unbiblical which is what the Hebrew Israelites are doing. **The Apostle Paul dealt with such people who were called 'Judaizers.'** For your information, **'Judaizers' were some 'Jewish Christians' who regarded the Levitical Laws of the Old Testament as still binding on all Christians.** Biblically speaking, they were in error. If you want to correct erroneous teaching and be well grounded in sound biblical doctrines, study the Books of Romans, Galatians and Hebrews.

No matter what one preaches or teaches about Salvation, Jesus Christ must be preeminent in the message concerning the things of God. In contrast, the Hebrew Israelites make the message of God about themselves instead of Jesus Christ; which raises a red flag. Hopefully, after reading this book, you will have a good understanding of the Gospel of Jesus Christ and how He fulfilled all the righteous requirements of the Law. As Christians, we must understand the importance of what we believe and why we believe it. This will equip every Christian to know how to defend what he believes.

The Hebrew Israelites' interpretation of the Bible is wrong because they do not realize that Jesus Christ is a 'Mystery' hidden in the Old Testament but is revealed in the New Testament. It is this ignorance that is at the core of their teachings and it makes them to believe that they are justified or saved by keeping the Law. This book goes into great details about this erroneous belief and teaching.

It is too bad that many professing Christians have not been properly grounded in the Christian Faith and it is why they go to churches with no **Solid Foundation** about what it means to be a Christian. There are a lot of popular preachers that preach a different Gospel other than the one the Apostles preached and it is why the Apostle Paul said in **Galatians 1: 6-8:**

> "6 **I marvel that** <u>ye are so soon removed from</u> <u>him that called you into the grace of Christ</u> <u>unto another gospel</u>: 7 Which is not another; but there be some that trouble you, and would pervert the gospel of Christ. 8 **But though we, or an angel from heaven, preach any other gospel unto you than that which we have preached unto you,** <u>let him be accursed.</u>"

As you just read from the scriptures above, those who are preaching a different Jesus other than the one that is in the Bible are under a curse. That is why it is important to be rooted and grounded in God's Truth in order to recognize what is not true or false.

The Hebrew Israelites are aggressively evangelizing Christian believers because they claim that there is something wrong with the Christian Faith. **Many people are judging Christianity based on the actions of some of the devil's children that profess to be Christians but are wolves in sheep clothing.** They base their slanders of the Christian Faith on the misguided actions of these wolves. Always remember that Satan is a slanderer and so are those following him; whether knowingly or unknowingly.

One of Satan's tactics is to attack the human mind with his lies in order to deceive people just as he did Eve in the Garden of Eden. His lies have some truth in them which makes them so dangerous because he twists the Word of God. Therefore, you must always remember that God's Truth does not have lies mixed up in it. I will illustrate this fact with the truth about **Rat Poison**. Most people are not aware that **Rat Poison** is made up of **99.9%** good food and only **.01%** is **Poison**. Please, remember this when it comes to Satan's lies because a little lie can equally be deadly.

Therefore, it is important to find a church that believes in sound biblical doctrines, theology and discipleship. I believe that **Expository Preaching** and **Teaching** (sticking to the Bible) are needed for good Christian growth. **We all must have our mind made up to be "Doers of the Word and not Hearers only." The Holy Spirit empowers and enables us to be obedient to God's Word when we choose to be Doers of the Word.** Therefore, we must depend on the Holy Spirit moment by moment. This is what is missing in the Hebrew Israelites' movement because **they are trying to please God in the flesh** which is impossible to do.

Foreword

The Bible tells us that there are times and seasons for everything (Eccl. 3). Thankfully, the Word of God never changes. The Black Hebrew Israelites cult has arisen in the United States to address what they have said are some perceived grievances and purposes. As a cult exclusively identified by ethnicity and physical appearances, the Black Hebrew Israelites claim to find their existential cues from the Old Testament. The Black Hebrew Israelites (BHI) point to the Hebrew scripture as their own; written by them and for them, but somehow stolen from them by another ethnic group by nefarious means. Their attempt is to reclaim an identification they believe to be rightfully theirs.

This seems to be at the center of why they exist. This identification or misidentification goes to the heart of the African-American slave-Diaspora: *who are we now as a people and why were our ancestors brought to American shores as slaves in the first place?* Every African-American since that time has had to struggle with the reverberations of slavery and its social and economic consequences. The fact is, such questions are difficult to sum up in a neat hypothesis and story. The challenge of the Black Hebrew Israelites is to make a believable *biblical and theological* story out of the African-American experience and somehow root those stories as facts into the Hebrew scriptures of the Bible. It is a tall order to which the Black Hebrew Israelites have concocted as a tall tale.

A twin challenge of the BHI is that of displacement or replacement. Their own claim of exclusive ethnic identification raises the question of who then are "real" Hebrews or why does it matter in Christ? If ethnicity is somehow a marker of specialness, what are we to make of "neither Jew nor Greek" (Col. 3:11) and many other passages in the New Testament which urge believers to look past such appearances? The BHI have to somehow replace not just a racial identity as their own but undertake a wholesale replacement of thousands of years of orthodox scriptural interpretation. This is not to say something like this has not been tried before. However, groups attempting to pigeon-hole such a narrow interpretation of their own theology into the Bible have been rightfully called cults.

The Bible encourages believers to defend the faith and integrity of the scriptures with fear and trembling (1 Peter 3:15). Alongside that admonition is the call to skillfully interpret the scriptures (2 Tim. 2:15). **Minister Carlton Green has been an able defender of the faith for over 30 years as a speaker, evangelist, urban missionary, and Christian apologist.** In this thoroughly researched book, he points to the shortcomings of the scriptural interpretation used by the BHI cult. He delves into the lies at the root of the BHI movement and lays bare the truth of how the Word of God has been misapplied by this group. The Bible tells us there will be no shortages of cults and false prophets and we clearly see this manifesting in our days. Their deception lies in what they appear to be and not who they really are. Thankfully, men like Minister Carlton Green have been there and faithfully stand at the watchman's tower to warn the people of God about the danger posed by such groups and exposing their plots to infiltrate God's flock.

— **Fred W. Ball, Jr., Ph.D.**
Educator & Christian Apologist

Table of Contents

Chapter 1
Ministering the Gospel Without the Holy Spirit

We all need the Spirit of God in order to understand the things of God but many people are trying to speak on behalf of God and the Bible without even being Christians; without having the Spirit of God. This has become a problem because **many professing Christians do not know Jesus Christ by His Spirit in their personal lives;** they are walking by the flesh.

Those in the Flesh Do Not Know God
We are told the following in **Romans 8:9:**

> "...**Now if any man have not the Spirit of Christ, he is none of his.**"

This is why it is very important to understand that the natural man (the unsaved person) cannot understand the things of God because according to scriptures in **1 Corinthians 2:10-14,** they are spiritually discerned:

> "10 But **God hath revealed them unto us by his Spirit: for the Spirit searcheth all things, yea, the deep things of God.** 11 For what man knoweth the things of a man, save the spirit of man which is in him? **even so the things of God knoweth no man, but the Spirit of God.** 12 Now **we have received, not the spirit of the world, but the spirit which is of God; that <u>we might know the things that are freely given to us of God.</u>**

13 Which things also we speak, not in the words which man's wisdom teacheth, but **which the Holy Ghost teacheth;** comparing **spiritual things with spiritual.**14 But **the natural man receiveth not the things of the Spirit of God**: for they are foolishness unto him: neither can he know them, because **they are spiritually discerned**."

It is also very important to be rooted, grounded and be able to rightly divide the Word of God (the Bible). The reason for this is because the enemy of our souls loves to deceive the minds of men. As I said before, this is a problem with professing Christians who do not know the Word of God and as a result, are targeted by cultists and shrewd believers in false doctrines. It is important as Christians to know what we believe and why we believe it. Below are some basic doctrines that we as Christians must believe with no exceptions in order to be a **True follower of Jesus Christ:**

1. The **Deity of Jesus Christ**
2. The **Doctrine of the Trinity**
3. The **Infallibility** or **Inerrancy of the Bible**
4. The **Virgin Birth of Jesus Christ**
5. The **Fall of Mankind in Adam**
6. **Man's Need of a Rebirth** (Regeneration)
7. The **Second Coming of Jesus Christ in the Flesh**

The above doctrines or beliefs are what the enemy of our soul attacks the most. This is the same way he attacked our first parents Adam and Eve in the Garden of Eden.

How the Devil Deceived Eve with Lies

Eve was approached by the serpent with a tactic that he is still using to this very day. The serpent started off the conversation by asking the following question in **Genesis 3:1**:

> "Now the serpent was more subtil than any beast of the field which the LORD God had made. And he said unto the woman, **Yea, hath God said, Ye shall not eat of every tree of the garden?**"

Eve's response to the serpent about the **Tree of the Knowledge of Good and Evil** was slightly different from what God told Adam. **Eve added to it by saying the word touch, but she did say the word die referring to eating the fruit thereof** — Genesis 3:2-4:

> "2 And the woman said unto the serpent, We may eat of the fruit of the trees of the garden: 3 But of the fruit of the tree which is in the midst of the garden, God hath said, **Ye shall not eat of it, neither shall ye touch it, lest ye die.** 4 And the serpent said unto the woman, **Ye shall not surely die**..."

The serpent then responded by denying God's Word and lied to Eve that she would not die if she disobeyed God and ate the fruit from the Tree of the Knowledge of Good and Evil. Then, the serpent replaced God's Word with his lie by saying, that God knows that if she ate the fruit her eyes would open and she would become as "gods" knowing both good and evil. Eve's eyes were not open until Adam ate the fruit and their eyes were open and they realized they were naked. I said all of this to get to this point concerning how the devil uses his lying tactics:

1. He **questions** God's Word
2. He **denies** God's Word
3. He **replaces** God's Word with his lies

These are the tactics used by the enemies of Christianity; the enemy of our soul. Note that the people representing false religions and the occultists usually approach Christians with these same tactics because the wicked one has taken them captives with his lies and deceptions.

The Purpose of this Book

My purpose for writing this book is to give the reader a true and accurate understanding of the Old Testament so those who are caught up in the movement called the 'Black Hebrew Israelites' or 'Hebrew Israelites' may know the truth of the Word of God. This is because the Hebrew Israelites **really believe** that what they ascribe to or believe is the Truth. They remind me of what the scriptures says in **Romans 10:2-4:**

"2 For I bear them record that **they have a zeal of God, but not according to knowledge.** 3 For they **being ignorant of God's righteousness, and going about to establish their own righteousness,** have not submitted themselves unto the righteousness of God. 4 For **Christ is the end of the law for righteousness** to everyone that believeth."

The Hebrew Israelites are operating with a zeal without knowledge. Therefore, true Christians should be mindful of the fact that we are 'behind enemy lines' when dealing with such erroneous beliefs. What I mean by this is that, we are in the world but not of the world. We are strangers and pilgrims passing through this life:

> "If ye were of the world, the world would love his own: **but because ye are not of the world,** but **I have chosen you out of the world,** therefore the world hateth you" (John 15:19)."

Chapter 2
The Law Has Not Been Done Away With

The Hebrew Israelites' Accusation against Christians

The Hebrew Israelites accuse Christians of teaching that the Law has been done away with. This statement is not true because, the Law has not been done away with. The Christian belief in the strength of the Law is explained by the Apostle Paul when he compared the Law and Christians to a Husband and Wife relationship; the Law is seen as the husband and Christians as the wife. In this relationship, if the husband lives, the wife is bound to her husband but if the husband dies, the wife is free to marry another. We see this in **Romans 7:1-4**:

> "1 Know ye not, brethren, (for I speak to them that know the law,) how that the law hath dominion over a man as long as he liveth? 2 **For the woman which hath an husband is bound by the law to her husband so long as he liveth; but if the husband be dead, she is loosed from the law of her husband.**
>
> 3 So then if, while her husband liveth, she be married to another man, she shall be called an adulteress: but if her husband be dead, she is free from that law; so that she is no adulteress, though she be married to another man. 4 Wherefore, my brethren, ye also are become dead to the law by the body of Christ; that ye should be married to another, even to him who is raised from the dead, that we should bring forth fruit unto God."

This is a beautiful truth that is revealed in the above verses. **The Law did not die, but we died in Christ Jesus and were raised with Him. Therefore, we are free to marry another even Jesus Christ Himself.** Know this, the Church (the body of believers in Christ Jesus) is called the **Bride of Christ**. This truth should bring joy to your heart.

The Hebrew Israelites Live by the Law

The Hebrew Israelites do not understand that if they live by the Law, they are bound by the Law to keep all of the Law which **no one can do** because the Law condemns them to death as we see in **Galatians 3:10:**

> "For **as many as are of the works of the law are under the curse:** for it is written, **Cursed is every one that continueth not in all things which are written in the book of the law to do them.**"

We are also told in **Romans 6:23** that the wages, of sin is death:

> "For the **wages of sin is death;** but **the gift of God is eternal life** through Jesus Christ our Lord."

Thank God that we Christians are free from the **Law of sin and death. We are set free by the Death and Resurrection of Jesus Christ with the promise of Eternal Life at the moment we believed by faith.** This is something to shout about and rejoice over; Hallelujah! It is why the Gospel of Jesus Christ is "Good News." You can say that God acquitted the Christians and never to bring up our sins and trespasses again; they have been thrown into the sea of forgetfulness. For this Lord Jesus, we are so forever thankful and grateful to You.

Chapter 3
Jesus Christ Fulfilled the Law

Hebrew Israelites' Misinterpretation of the Law

The Hebrew Israelites' interpretation of the Bible is based on their view of themselves **who are not descendants of Abraham** as God's chosen people for Salvation because of their **Race** and **Birthright**. They believe that Jesus Christ, whom they call **Yahushua Hamashiach** came to save His people (them) from their sins. **The truth is that what the Lord Jesus said was meant for both <u>Jewish people</u> and the <u>Gentiles</u> whom He viewed as both His people.** He meant all those who would put their faith and trust in Him as their Savior for the Salvation of their souls. The error is that the Hebrew Israelites' misinterpretation of the scriptures comes from their emphasizing the Old Testament scriptures over the New Testament scriptures.

For example, they teach that the New Testament scriptures are to be **discarded** if they contradict their narrative (man's opinion). **Their understanding of the Old Testament is wrong because they try to make the New Testament scriptures fit their social and cultural opinion of who they are. Meaning, that they superimpose their opinion of themselves on the Word of God thereby seeing themselves as God's only chosen people!** This view is the result of their violation of the principles of Hermeneutics. <u>**In other words, to properly expound or interpret scriptures, they must stay true to the scriptural context and with the rest of the scriptures.**</u> The basic principle of Hermeneutics is Context, Context and Context! What this means is that, every verse in the Bible is in a chapter, the chapter is in a book, and the book is in the Bible which consists of 66 Books. **Therefore, your interpretation of a biblical truth must harmonize with the other Books of the Bible without contradicting them.**

The Bible Does Not Contradict Itself

Let us now look at some verses of scriptures that are used by the Hebrew Israelites to make their point about their beliefs. The first verse we will look at is **John 4:22** where Jesus said that, "**Salvation is of the Jews;**" which simply means **that Salvation comes through the Jews.** The **Hebrew Israelites have put themselves in place of Jesus Christ in whom Salvation is obtained by through faith.** Jesus Christ is from the **Tribe of Juda** being one of the 12 tribes of Israel. The Old Testament scriptures point to this truth.

Remember that the Bible does not contradict itself. The very first prophecy concerning the Messiah; Jesus Christ, is found in **Genesis 3:15**, concerning the Seed of the woman crushing the serpent's head and the serpent bruising His heel:

> "And **I will put enmity between thee and the woman, <u>and between thy seed and her seed</u>; <u>it shall bruise thy head</u>, and <u>thou shalt bruise his heel</u>.**"

Their Misunderstanding about the Seed of the Woman

This verse above is saying a lot concerning **the Seed of the woman being someone who is fully human and who is later identified as <u>a man with</u>**

<u>the power to the destroy devil</u> which is depicted as a serpent in the Garden of Eden. We know that only God has the power to destroy the devil. **Therefore, this man would have to be fully man and fully God at the same time.** This is why the Lord Jesus Christ is known in Theological Circles as the **Theos-Anthropos**; the **God Man. The Deity of Jesus Christ is the central foundation of the Christian Faith.**

We will now look at another text of scripture referencing the Messiah; Jesus Christ in **Genesis 22:16-18** where God tells Abraham that through his seed all nations (families) of the earth shall be blessed.

> "16 And said, **By myself have I sworn, saith the LORD,** for because thou hast done this thing, and hast not withheld thy son, thine only son: 17 **That in blessing I will bless thee, and in multiplying I will multiply thy seed as the stars of the heaven,** and as the sand which is upon the sea shore; and thy seed shall possess the gate of his enemies; 18 <u>**And in thy seed shall all the nations of the earth be blessed**</u>; because thou hast obeyed my voice."

The Hebrew Israelites view themselves as this Seed of Abraham which happens to be a false view. The correct view is seen in **Galatians 3:16** where Jesus Christ is said to be the Seed of Abraham.

> "Now to Abraham and his seed were the promises made. He saith not, And to seeds, as of **many**; but as of one, **And to thy seed, which is Christ.**"

As you can read in the above scriptures, it clearly states that the word **Seed** is singular and that it refers to **Jesus Christ** and not seeds as of many. This truth is again stated in **Galatians 3:29,** where it says that **those who have faith in Jesus Christ are truly Abraham's Seed and heirs** according to the promise. **It is by faith in Jesus Christ that makes us the Seed of Abraham and not by Race or Birthright:**

"And **if ye be Christ's, then are ye Abraham's seed, and heirs** according to the promise."

God's Promise to Abraham and His Descendants

God also made a promise to Abraham's son Isaac and his grandson Jacob and God changed Jacob's name to Israel. Jacob had 12 sons. Concerning the lineage of Jesus Christ, God ordained that Israel's son **Juda** would be the one the Messiah Jesus Christ would come through. Later, God made the same promise to **King David** who was also from the Tribe of Juda that the Messiah Jesus Christ would come; the seed of King David. In fulfillment of His promise, God will make Christ to sit on the Throne of David in Jerusalem forever—**2 Samuel 7:12-16:**

"12 And when thy days be fulfilled, and thou shalt sleep with thy fathers, **I will set up thy seed after thee, which shall proceed out of thy bowels, and I will establish his kingdom.** 13 **He shall build an house for my name, and I will stablish the throne of his kingdom forever.** 14 **I will be his father, and he shall be my son…** 15 But my mercy shall not depart away from him, as I took it from Saul, whom

I put away before thee. 16 **And thine house and thy kingdom shall be established forever before thee: thy throne shall be established forever.**"

Prophecy about the Messiah and His Everlasting Kingdom

The prophecy concerning the **Messiah Jesus Christ's coming to save His people** and **the world from sins** and establishing a **Kingdom** in Israel is also in **Isaiah 9:2-7:**

> "The people that walked in darkness have seen a great light: they that dwell in the land of the shadow of death, upon them hath the light shined... 6 **For unto us a child is born, unto us a son is given:** and **the government shall be upon his shoulder:** and **his name shall be called** Wonderful, Counsellor, The mighty God, The everlasting Father, The Prince of Peace. 7 **Of the increase of his government and peace there shall be no end, upon the throne of David,** and **upon his kingdom,** to order it, **and to establish it with judgment and with justice from henceforth even forever.** The zeal of the LORD of hosts will perform this."

The Hebrew Israelites see themselves as the only ones that this prophecy above is referring to. Knowing who God's chosen people (the Elect) really are; the Jews, it is very important to point out this false view. **God's chosen people are both the Jews and Gentiles who have been made one by their faith Jesus Christ.** On the contrary, the Hebrew Israelites believe that **the Gentiles cannot be saved unless they <u>submit themselves to the traditions</u> of the Hebrew Israelites;** their traditions. This view is not biblical.

They do not understand that the New Testament is the Old Testament revealed in Christ. **Jesus Christ was a Mystery in the Old Testament that is now revealed to those who have put their faith in Him.** The Holy Spirit dwells inside the true believers. He is the witness which testifies in us that Jesus Christ is Lord and that God raised Him from the dead. The Holy Spirit bears witness in Heaven and in the earth —**1 John 5:7-8:**

> "**7 For there are three that bear record in heaven, the Father, the Word, and the Holy Ghost**: and **these three are one.** *8* And **there are three that bear witness in earth, the Spirit, and the water, and the blood**: and **these three agree in one**."

Also, the Holy Spirit bears witness with our regenerated spirit that we are the children of God as written in **Romans 8:16:**

> "The Spirit **itself beareth witness with our spirit**, that we are the children of God."

Other Instances of Contradictions in Hebrew Israelites Teachings

As I said before, the Hebrew Israelites are taught that if any New Testament scripture contradicts their understanding of the Old Testament, they are to **discard** it. Again, remember that the Bible does not contradict itself because **all scripture is God breathed.** This is why it is stated in **2 Timothy 3:16-17** that, scriptures are profitable for doctrine, reproof, correction and instruction in righteousness in order that the man of God is thoroughly equipped;

rightly dividing the Word of God (having a correct understanding) removes erroneous teachings:

> *"16* **All scripture is given by** inspiration **of God**, and is profitable for doctrine, for reproof, for correction, for instruction in righteousness: *17* **That the man of God may be perfect, throughly furnished unto all good works.***"*

Jews and Gentiles Receive the Baptism of the Holy Spirit

We are going to look at some more New Testament scriptures that contradict the false teachings of the Hebrew Israelites. These scriptures give a full understanding of the Gospel of Jesus Christ. For example, in **Acts 10:1-48**, there is a situation concerning a **Roman Centurion by the name of Cornelius**; a Gentile who was justified by his faith. When he sent for the Apostle Peter to hear the Word of God, Peter admitted to him in **verses 34-36** that God has chosen unto Himself a people that believe in Jesus Christ. As a result, Cornelius and his whole household believed and were baptized:

> *"34* Then Peter opened his mouth, and said, Of a truth I perceive that **God is no respecter of persons**: *35* But in every nation he that feareth him, and worketh righteousness, is accepted with him. *36* The word which God sent unto the children of Israel, preaching peace by Jesus Christ: (he is Lord of all.)*"*

If you notice, the Apostle Peter witnessed before many Jews that **whosoever believes in Jesus Christ is justified by God** because God is not a respecter of persons. While Peter was speaking, the Holy Spirit fell upon Cornelius and his family just as on the Day of Pentecost when all the believers in the Upper Room were baptized.

Another text of scripture referencing both Jews and Gentiles being justified by God is Romans chapters 1, 2 and 3 where the Apostle Paul is teaching that believers are justified by faith in Jesus Christ and not by keeping the Law of Moses — **Romans 3:28:**

> "Therefore we **conclude that a man is justified by faith without the deeds of the law**."

When you read all 3 chapters listed above, you will see that Paul called **the Gentiles** into God's Courtroom and declared them all guilty before God. Also, Paul called **the Jews** into God's Courtroom and declared them equally guilty before God even though the Jews were the ones that God gave the Law, the Commandments, the Covenants and Promises; **they were the custodians of God's Law and Promise!**

In other words, Paul declared both **Jews** and **Gentiles** guilty before God. He goes further in Romans chapter 3 and **declares the whole world guilty before God**; both Jews and Gentiles. We read **Romans 3:23** which says, **"For all have sinned and fall short of the glory of God."** <u>Sin means to miss the Mark of God's Holy Perfection</u>. In order to be declared righteous enough to spend Eternity with Him in Heaven forever, you must believe in His Son Jesus Christ.

Other scriptures that contradict the teachings of the Hebrew Israelites are found in **Acts 20:21** which says that both Greeks and Jews are justified by faith in Jesus Christ. Also, in **Acts 28:25-28** in which the Paul writes about the sin of unbelief by the Jews and **how God's Salvation would be offered to the Gentiles because the Gentiles would believe; they will be accepted through faith** as we see below:

> "25 And when they agreed not among themselves, they departed, after that Paul had spoken one word, Well spake the Holy Ghost by Esaias the prophet unto our fathers, 26 Saying, **Go unto this people, and say, Hearing ye shall hear, and shall not understand; and seeing ye shall see, and not perceive:** 27 **For the heart of this people is waxed gross, and their ears are dull of hearing, and their eyes have they closed;** lest they should see with their eyes, and hear with their ears, and understand with their heart, and should be converted, and I should heal them. 28 **Be it known therefore unto you, that the salvation of God is sent unto the Gentiles, and that they will hear it**."

This message is repeated throughout the New Testament but remember that according to the Hebrew Israelites, these scriptures, these truths in the scripture are to be discarded because they contradict their false narratives as they insist on holding on to their misunderstanding of the Old Testament.

The First Thing that the Hebrew Israelites Lack

The Hebrew Israelites are missing two very important criteria for Salvation. They are **lacking the Holy Spirit** and you can tell it by their **lack of the fruit**

of the Spirit; there is no 'Agape' meaning that, they lack the 'God kind of love' (Agape) in their ministry. Paul writes in **Ephesians 4:15** that, "We speak the truth in love" and also in **1 Timothy 1:7-11,** he says the following about those who insist on living only by the Law:

> "*7* Desiring to be teachers of the law; understanding neither what they say, nor whereof they affirm. *8* **But we know that the law is good, if a man use it lawfully;** *9* Knowing this, that **the law is not made for a righteous man, but for the lawless and disobedient, for** the **ungodly and for sinners**, for unholy and profane, for murderers of fathers and murderers of mothers, for manslayers, *10* For whoremongers, for them that defile themselves with mankind, for menstealers, for liars, for perjured persons, and if there be any other thing that is contrary to sound doctrine; *11* According to the glorious gospel of the blessed God, which was committed to my trust."

As you can see, the Apostle Paul painted a clear picture that fits the Hebrew Israelites perfectly in the above scriptures. I pray that you the reader will avoid this serious error by the Hebrew Israelites. The One True and Only Living God means business when it comes to His Word. **In order to have the Holy Spirit, one must be Born Again or born from above**. Being Born Again must be a reality in your life and not head knowledge. Otherwise, your belief is a counterfeit faith which makes you a **Reprobate**. To be a **Reprobate** means to be condemned by God or to be disproven by God. The Bible talks about a reprobate mind in **Romans 1:28:**

"And even **as they did not like to retain God in their knowledge, God gave them over to a reprobate mind**, to do those things which are not convenient..."

The Second Thing the Hebrew Israelites Lack

The second criteria that the Hebrew Israelites lack is a **full understanding of the Gospel of Jesus Christ.** They misunderstood what the Lord Jesus meant when He said that He did not come to destroy the Law or the prophets, but to fulfill it. **The Lord Jesus Christ was born under the Law and he lived a perfect life without committing sin even one time! He met all of the righteous requirements of the Law and then offered Himself as sin sacrifice in our place on the Cross;** He died a real death. Yes, **1 of the 3 Persons in the Godhead died a real death** and was raised from the dead for the justification of the Christians who place their faith in Him –**Romans 4:25:**

"**Who was delivered for our offences**, and **was raised again for our justification**."

The Apostle Paul taught in the Book of Romans that believers in Jesus Christ are in fact, perfectly fulfilling the Law because they are justified by faith before God who has imputed Jesus Christ's righteousness to their account. This is a legal transaction that is done by God Himself and it is why **there is no condemnation to those who are in Christ**. On the other hand, the Hebrew Israelites have no 'good news' because they believe that they will inherit Salvation by keeping the Law, keeping the Sabbath Days along with the Feast Days in Leviticus 23. This belief is not scriptural and therefore, is not true. The Bible states in **Romans 3:20** that by the works of the Law, no flesh (Human Being) shall be justified in His sight; meaning in God's sight.

They Believe the Law has Been Done Away with

The Hebrew Israelites also **misrepresent Christianity** by saying that Christians teach that the Law or the Old Testament has been done away with. The Hebrew Israelites really believe that they have the truth of God's Word to the point that they have started to challenge the Christian faith in churches across the nation. This is one reason why it is very important for Christians to get a good understanding of the Old and the New Testaments so that they can effectively answer the lies and errors of the Hebrew Israelite when they encounter them; they must be able to state and defend what is in the Bible.

God's truth (His Word) is absolute which means that it is true whether you believe it or not; it stands as His truth forever. Also, God never changes and He is immutable. The word **immutable** means **unchanged over a period, or unable to be changed.** This is why the immutability of God is one of His attributes. God is faithful to keep all His promises that He made to Abraham, Isaac and Jacob. Jesus Christ is the fulfillment of these promises. Faithfulness is another attribute of the immutable character of God.

Romans 8:8 tells us that those that are in the flesh cannot please God. Man's attempt to please God in the flesh by keeping the Law, the Sabbath Days and Feast Days is useless. Jesus Christ took care of all those things within Himself. When it comes to Salvation for Christians, Jesus cried from the Cross that, "**It is**

finished" in John 19:30. God's plan of redeeming man back to Himself was accomplished by Jesus Christ. The **first Adam fell** and all humanity fell with him but the **Last Adam (Jesus Christ) was successful** — **1 Corinthians 15:42-49:**

"42 So also is **the resurrection of the dead.** It is sown in corruption; it is raised in incorruption: 43 It is sown in dishonour; it is raised in glory: it is sown in weakness; it is raised in power: 44 It is sown a natural body; it is raised a spiritual body. There is a natural body, and there is a spiritual body. 45 And so it is written, **The first man Adam was made a living soul;** <u>the last Adam (Jesus Christ) was made a quickening spirit.</u>

46 Howbeit that was not first which is spiritual, but that which is natural; and afterward that which is spiritual. 47 **The first man is of the earth, earthy:** <u>the second man is the Lord from heaven</u>. 48 As is the earthy, such are they also that are earthy: and as is the heavenly, such are they also that are heavenly. 49 **And as we have borne the image of the earthy, we shall also bear the image of the heavenly."**

Chapter 4
The Tabernacle and Jesus Christ

The Tabernacle known as the Tabernacle of Moses was built in the wilderness during the children of Israel's journey from Egypt to the Promise Land. If you have not done so yet, I encourage you to do a study on the **Tabernacle** because you will see how the workings of the Tabernacle are fulfilled in Jesus Christ Himself. It will bless you but I will cover some of those fulfilments at this time.

The Entrance into the Tabernacle
The Tabernacle had <u>only one entrance</u> and it fulfills the fact that <u>Jesus Christ is the Only Way</u> to the Father as He stated in **John 14:6:**

"Jesus saith unto him, **I am the way, the truth, and the life: no man cometh unto the** Father, **but by me.**"

Also, there is <u>only one Mediator</u> between God and man and that is Jesus Christ— 1 Timothy 2:5-6:

"**For** there **is one God, and one mediator between God and men, the man Christ Jesus;** 6 Who gave himself a ransom for all, to be testified in due time."

The Contents in the Tabernacle
The Alter of Sacrifice
The <u>first piece of furniture</u> the worshipers would approach was the **Altar of Sacrifice**. This is where the Levitical Priest would perform the animal sacrifices

for sin offerings. **In Hebrews 7:11-17, Jesus Christ is revealed as a Priest after the Order of Melchizedek; pointing to the superiority of the Priesthood of Christ over the Priesthood of men on the earth.** Christ priesthood is in Heaven where God's real Tabernacle is. It is this heavenly Tabernacle that the one Moses built on earth was patterned after:

> "*11* If therefore perfection were by the Levitical priesthood, (for under it the people received the law,) what further need was there that another priest should rise after the order of Melchisedec, and not be called after the order of Aaron? *12* **For the priesthood being changed, there is made of necessity a change also of the law.** *13* For he (Jesus) of whom these things are spoken pertaineth to another tribe, of which no man gave attendance at the altar.
>
> *14* **For it is evident that our Lord sprang out of Juda; of which tribe Moses spake nothing concerning priesthood. *15* And it is yet far more evident: for that after the similitude of Melchisedec there ariseth another priest, *16* Who is made, not after the law of a carnal commandment, but after the power of an endless life.** *17* For he testifieth, Thou art a priest for ever after the order of Melchisedec."

Jesus Christ as the Great High Priest offered Himself up to God for a sin sacrifice once and for all.

The Lever for Washing

The **second piece of furniture** was the **Laver used by the priests who were from the Tribe of Levi to**

wash the animal sacrifices. This was fulfilled in Jesus when John the Baptist who was a Levite and of the house of Aaron baptized Him. **John then introduced Jesus as "the Lamb of God who takes away the sins of the world."** The fact is that, John the Baptist's parents were from the Tribe of Levi and the house of Aaron and this **qualified John the Baptist to** wash Jesus as the 'Sin Sacrifice.' This is why the Lord Jesus told John the Baptist that their actions would be fulfilling all righteousness before John baptized Him. We see this in **Matthew 3:13-17:**

"13 Then cometh Jesus from Galilee to Jordan unto John, to be baptized of him. 14 **But John forbad him, saying, I have need to be baptized of thee, and comest thou to me?** 15 **And Jesus answering said unto him, Suffer it to be so now: for thus it becometh us to fulfil all righteousness.** Then he suffered him. 16 And Jesus, when he was baptized, went up straightway out of the water: and, lo, the heavens were opened unto him, and he saw the Spirit of God descending like a dove, and lighting upon him: 17 And lo a voice from heaven, saying, This is my beloved Son, in whom I am well pleased."

The Lampstand

Another piece of furniture inside the Tabernacle is called, **the Lampstand** with 7 branches. The **Lampstand was the only source of light inside the Tabernacle. This is fulfilled in Jesus Christ when He identified Himself as being the "Light of World."** The Holy Spirit who is also called the **Spirit of Christ** is seen in scriptures as having **7 spirits**. Just as the Lampstand is the only source of illumination inside the Tabernacle, **the Holy Spirit is the only source of illumination in the Christian's heart and mind when it comes to learning about the things of God.**

The Table of Shewbread

Opposite the Lampstand was the **Table of Shewbread** with 12 cakes of bread on it at all times. Jesus Christ fulfilled this piece of furniture by being born in Bethlehem. The word **Bethlehem** means **House of Bread** and Jesus Christ proclaimed Himself as **"The Bread of Life."** These examples are all part of understanding the Gospel of Jesus Christ. Understanding the meaning of these pieces of furniture in the Tabernacle is also lacking in what the Hebrew Israelites teach.

Carrying the Tabernacle

It is very important not just to know what a text of scripture says, but what it means. The Tabernacle had to be taken apart and carried by the Tribe of Levi when all the Tribes of Israel moved from place to place. Jesus Christs' fulfillment of this aspect of the Tabernacle is also very significant; **believers carry the Lord everywhere they go.** The Gospel of **John 1:1** says, "In the beginning was the Word, and the Word was with God and the Word was God." This verse is referring to the **Deity of Jesus Christ** and in **John 1:14** it says, "The Word was made flesh and dwelt among us."

This verse is referring to the **Incarnation of Jesus Christ**. The word **dwelt** is **translated** as **Tabernacled. Yes, the Tabernacle is now walking among men with no need to be carried about by the Tribe of Levi!** Before the Cross, Jesus Christ the Tabernacle of God lived among men and walked under the Law but the Law could not condemn Him as it condemns us. The Tabernacle of God (Jesus Christ) also ministered the Word of God directly to men with Authority from God alone. This is the truth in scriptures being laid out in front of you.

They Usurp the Position of Christ

The Hebrew Israelites put themselves in place of Jesus Christ as the Seed of Abraham in whom all the families of the earth would be blessed. This act alone disqualifies them as representatives of God and they have many other fallible acts and doctrines. The Lord Jesus referred to the Pharisees as "blind leaders of the blind." The Black Hebrew Israelites are just like modern day Pharisees who stumble over the same stone (Jesus Christ) as the Pharisees did during the time of Jesus' earthly ministry. Somethings seem to repeat themselves throughout history.

Chapter 5
Is Christianity of European Origin?

Origin of the Name 'Christians'
The Hebrew Israelites claim that the message of Christianity is of European origin and they think that they can use their unbiblical message to discredit Christianity. The word **Christian** was first mentioned in the Bible in **Acts 11:25-26** where the **disciples were first called "Christians" at Antioch**; this also referred to disciples that were in Jerusalem:

> "25 Then departed Barnabas to Tarsus, for to seek Saul: 26 And when he had found him, he brought him unto Antioch. And it came to pass, that a whole year they assembled themselves with the church, and taught much people. **And the disciples were called Christians first in Antioch.**"

Before the disciples were called Christians at Antioch, they were called "The Way." God is seeking people to worship Him in Spirit and in Truth. Meaning that, God wants a relationship through His Spirit. Remember that those who are in the flesh cannot please God. That is why one must be Born Again or Born from above by the Spirit of God by faith in Jesus Christ.

The New Testament Reveals
the Old Testament
We have to remember that **the Old Testament is the New Testament concealed and the New Testament is the Old Testament revealed.** A good comparison to this would be the Seed of an Oak Tree. The seed has the full potential of the tree, so when it is planted and

matures, an Oak Tree is revealed. **In the same way, Jesus Christ is a Mystery in the Old Testament that is now revealed in the New Testament.** Were Abraham, Isaac and Jacob of European origin? No; as a matter of fact, **of the 41 men who wrote the Bible, not one of them was European!**

An example of **God revealing a hidden truth in the Old Testament** is what happened on the **Day of Pentecost.** On this day, the **Holy Spirit** fell on the disciples **(Christians)** thereby fulfilling the Old Testament prophecy in **Joel 2:28** as written in **Acts 2:14-18:**

> "14 But Peter, standing up with the eleven, lifted up his voice, and said unto them, Ye men of Judaea, and all ye that dwell at Jerusalem, be this known unto you, and hearken to my words: 15 For these are not drunken, as ye suppose, seeing it is but the third hour of the day. 16 **But this is that which was spoken by the prophet Joel;** 17 **And it shall come to pass in the last days, saith God, I will pour out of my Spirit upon all flesh: and your sons and your daughters shall prophesy, and your young men shall see visions, and your old men shall dream dreams:** 18 **And on my servants and on my handmaidens I will pour out in those days of my Spirit; and they shall prophesy...**"

The Apostle Peter quoted the scriptures in Joel Chapter 2 of the Old Testament. In other words, what was written in the Old Testament was being revealed for all to see — **God's Spirit being poured out!**

Infiltration of the Church by Counterfeit Christians

Unfortunately, Church of Jesus Christ has been infiltrated by 'counterfeit Christians' and the Hebrew Israelites point to this. **They refer to the history of the United States at the time of slavery when 'counterfeit Christians' murdered millions upon millions of Africans and the Hebrew Israelites try to use this to discredit Christianity.** The Bible is very clear when it comes to hatred and murder, it says that those who commit them have no Eternal Life dwelling in them. **In other words, they are not Christians — 1 John 3:15:**

"Whosoever hateth his brother is a murderer: and **ye know that no murderer hath eternal life abiding in him.**"

True Bible believing Christians are followers of Jesus Christ and can anyone find fault in Jesus Christ? The Lord Jesus Christ said that a tree is known by the fruit it bears. For example, the fruit of hatred and murder are fruit from the devil's children. **You cannot use the devil's children to discredit God's children.**

The Hebrew Israelites' view of Christianity is wrong. It is painful to hear them spew out their hatred and ignorance. The fruit they are bearing is proof that they are not representing the God of the Bible. We are told in **1 John 4:7-8** that **God is love** and that **anyone who loves is born of God.** On the other hand, those that do not love are not born of God:

"7 Beloved, let us love one another: **for love is of God;** and **every one that loveth is born of God**, and knoweth God. 8 He that **loveth not** knoweth not God; for God is love."

Using Catholicism to Discredit Christianity

The Hebrew Israelites also point to the **Roman Catholic's Catholicism** (Roman pagan beliefs) as another means to discredit Christianity. **True believers know that Roman Catholicism is not Christianity; it is another Gospel that is under a curse.** The Catholic Church preaches another Jesus and not the Jesus of the Bible. It is an example of what the Apostle Paul warned us against in **2 Corinthians 11:4:**

> **"For if he that cometh preacheth another Jesus, whom we have not preached,** or if ye receive another spirit, which ye have not received, or another gospel, which ye have not accepted, ye might well bear with him."

And also, in **Galatians 1:8:**

> **"But though we, or an angel from heaven, preach any other gospel unto you than that which we have preached unto you, <u>let him be accursed</u>."**

It is not just the **Roman Catholic Church** that preaches another Gospel because there are some so called **Protestant Churches** that also preach a different Gospel and a false Christ.

Their Lies about the Origin of the Ethiopian Church

The Hebrew Israelites also make false reference about the origin of the Ethiopian Church. **The truth is that the Ethiopian Church was <u>founded by the Ethiopian Eunuch</u>** who was in Jerusalem on the Day of Pentecost and was baptized by the disciple called Philip in **Acts 8:26-40.** This Church never fell under the influence of the Roman Catholic Church or anything that is European. How can someone say that Christianity was created by Europeans without any supporting evidence? It was the 'Ethiopian Christianity' that influenced **Martin Luther** who is known as the **Great Reformer**.

This false narratives about Christianity being created by Europeans is based on their hatred and lies; the author of it is the devil himself who is the "father of lies." The worst type of a liar is someone who believes they are telling the truth. **Any group of people apart from the Jews who try to segregate themselves as Gods chosen people based on their race are biblically incorrect.** This is what the Hebrew Israelites are doing.

God's Hidden Mystery about the Salvation of Gentiles

The **Europeans** are called **Gentiles** in the Bible but the Hebrew Israelites call them **Edomites**; meanings, **descendants of Esau.** What does the Bible say about whether the Gentiles can be saved or be justified by God without submitting themselves to the Gospel of Jesus Christ? **Gentile can only be saved through Jesus Christ** as we see in **Ephesians 3:1-6:**

"1 For this cause I Paul, the prisoner of Jesus Christ for you Gentiles, 2 if ye have heard of the dispensation of the grace of God which is given me to you-ward: 3 How that by revelation he made known to the mystery; as I wrote afore in few words, 4 Whereby when you read, ye may understand my knowledge in the mystery of Christ 5 Which in other ages was not made known unto the sons of men, as it is now revealed unto his holy apostles and prophets by the Spirit; 6 **That <u>the Gentiles should be fellow heirs,</u> and of the same body, and <u>partakers of his promise in Christ by the gospel</u>"**

You saw earlier that in the Old Testament, Jesus Christ was a Mystery. This Mystery has now been made known and what is this Mystery? The **answer** is what we just read in the above scriptures, **"That the Gentiles should be fellow heirs, and of the same body, and partakers of God's promise in Christ by the Gospel."**

This is why the Apostle Paul warned Timothy about some men who were desiring to be teachers of the Law without understanding what they say or what they affirmed — **1Timothy 1:6-7:**

> "6 From which *(the Lord's commandments)* some **having swerved have turned aside unto vain jangling; 7 Desiring to be teachers of the law; <u>understanding neither what they say, nor whereof they affirm.</u>"**

This description fits the Hebrew Israelites perfectly because they regard themselves as God's exclusively chosen people and they misrepresent the Bible in their attempts to prove it. I once read somewhere that, "A false teacher exposes themselves by how they handle the Word of God" (the Bible).

The message of repentance toward God is for everyone meaning all races. Jesus said that, if He be lifted up, He would draw all men unto Himself. Know that "all men" does not mean that everyone will be saved, but that all 'types of men' meaning all races.

Chapter 6
Jesus Christ Fulfilled the Feast Days

The Feast Days in Leviticus Chapter 23 were fulfilled in Jesus Christ. In their opposition, the Hebrew Israelites claim that by keeping the Law, keeping the Sabbath days and the Feast days, they can obtain Salvation. They ignore the Word of God that says that Jesus Christ is the Lord's Salvation for all humanity. The Gospel of **Luke 2:25-30** confirms this:

> "25 And behold, there was a man in Jerusalem, whose name was Simeon; and same man was just and devout, **waiting for the consolation of Israel**: The Holy Ghost was upon him. 26 And it was revealed unto him by the Holy Ghost, that he should not see death, before he had seen the Lord's Christ. 27 And he came by the Spirit into the temple: and when the parents brought in the child Jesus, to do for him after the custom of the law, 28 **Then took he him up in his arms, and blessed God and said,** 29 **Lord now let thou thy servant depart in peace, according to thy word:** 30 **For mine eyes have seen thy salvation.**"

The Feast days in Leviticus 23 all ended on the first day of the week (meaning, the day after the Sabbath day) and Jesus Christ fulfilled the Feast Days within Himself. During the Feast days outlined in Leviticus 23, the first day of the week was observed as a Sabbath Day.

This is why Christians observed the first day of the week as the 'Lord's Day' and they come together for worship. I would encourage the reader to do an in-depth study on how Jesus Christ fulfilled the Feast days and how the Feasts are the 'Types' in the Old Testament concerning Jesus Christ. In other words, the feasts are speaking of **Jesus' Work of Salvation** for humanity.

Christ Fulfilled the Righteous Requirements of the Law

Jesus Christ met all the righteous requirements of the Law perfectly without committing an act of sin once! He is the only one who ever lived on earth to do so; no one else has kept the Law. If anyone says they have, they are lying. There is no Salvation in trying to keep the Law because the Bible says in several places that **by the deeds of law shall no flesh be justified in God's sight.** For example, take a look at **Romans 3:20-24**:

> "20 **Therefore by the deeds of the law there shall no flesh be justified in his sight: for by the law is the knowledge of sin.** 21 But now the righteousness of God without the law is manifested, being witnessed by the law and the prophets; 22 **Even the righteousness of God which is by faith of Jesus Christ unto all and upon all them that believe: for there is no difference**: 23 For <u>all have sinned</u>, and come short of the glory of God; 24 **Being justified freely by his grace through the redemption that is in Christ Jesus.**"

There is a saying, "The Law is not the Gospel, but the Gospel is not lawless." May the Lord bless the reader of this book with a better understanding of the Gospel of Jesus Christ.

Chapter 7
What Is Eisegesis?

Wrong Interpretation of Scriptures

The word **Eisegesis** means to **impose one's own interpretation, or narrative on a text of scripture to make it mean something other than what the text really means.** This is what the Hebrew Israelites are doing to the scriptures. You see, when one **eisegete or adds their own meaning to scriptures, <u>they can make the Bible say anything they want it to say</u>.** That is why it is very important to keep the scriptures in their proper context and to **get the real meaning of what is being said.**

The best type of preaching and teaching is 'Expository Preaching' and teaching; meaning teaching that incorporates the real meaning of what is being said in the text of the scripture. Therefore, it is important to study the Bible correctly and in so doing, you will be able to tell right away when someone is mishandling the scriptures. **The Bible does not contradict itself nor are scriptures to be discarded.** Many false movements started from **using eisegesis** when interpreting the Bible.

The U. S. Treasury Agents are trained to detect counterfeit money by **only studying real money to the point they get so familiar with real money** so that when counterfeit money appears, they immediately recognize it. Likewise, we are to get so familiar with God's Word throughout the scriptures so that when someone is using the scriptures out of context, we can immediately recognize it. We as Christians, have the Holy Spirit dwelling within us and He leads and guides us in God's truth.

I pray that this book will be helpful in equipping God's people and help them to be able to take a stand for God's truth. Also, I pray that God will use this book to show the Hebrew Israelites the error of their ways in Jesus name; Amen.

Chapter 8
Who Is Jesus Christ?

Jesus as Part of the Godhead

One of the essentials of the Christian Faith is **the Deity** of Jesus Christ. **This means that true Christians believe that Jesus Christ is One of the 3 Persons in the Godhead.** Jesus Christ is God in the Flesh which is also called the **Incarnation of Jesus Christ.** According to **John 1:1-3,** Jesus Christ was with God in the beginning. **It also states that all things were made by Him and that without Him was not anything made that was made:**

> "1 **In the beginning was the Word, and the Word was with God, and the Word was God.** 2 The same was in the beginning with God. 3 **All things were made by him; and without him was not anything made that was made.**"

Jesus Christ is God but not all by Himself because **God is 3 Distinct Persons,** yet one God. Even Jesus said that He came not to do His will but the will of the One who sent Him — **John 5:30:**

> "I can of mine own self do nothing: as I hear, I judge: and my judgment is just; because **I seek not <u>mine own will,</u> but <u>the will of the Father</u> which hath sent me.**"

Notice that there are 'two wills' mentioned in the above scriptures. <u>**Jesus's will**</u> and **<u>the Father's will</u>;** meaning, **2 Persons** right there.

The Doctrine of the Trinity

The doctrine of **Trinity** is the Christian belief that there are **3 Persons** in the **Godhead** but **One God.** This doctrine is an essential part of the Christian Faith but **it is constantly attacked by the enemy (satan) in his attempt to nullify the Deity of Jesus Christ.** This attack was popularized in early Church History by an Alexandrian priest named **Arius who taught people the denial of the Trinity and the Deity of Jesus Christ;** this teaching is called **Arianism.**

Therefore, Arianists believe that Jesus Christ was <u>created by God</u> and that He has <u>no coeternal existence with God the Father.</u> Examples of modern day Arianists would be the **Jehovah Witnesses** and the **Oneness Pentecostals.** I do not want to forget to point out that Jesus said that, **He came down from heaven** in **John 6:38.** Meaning that He was someplace else before coming to earth; no man can make this claim but Jesus:

"For **<u>I came down from heaven</u>, not to do mine own will, but the will of <u>him that sent me</u>.**"

The Solitariness of God

Genesis 1:1 says, "In the beginning **God** made the heavens and the earth." When you look at the **first four words in Genesis 1:1**, you will notice that <u>before</u> **God** created anything, there was **<u>only God</u>** and He was alone. In the theological circles, it is called the **Solitariness of God** and it is one of God's attributes. According to **John 1:1**, Jesus Christ was with God in the beginning. What man can make this claim other than Jesus?

The Deity of Jesus Christ

When Jesus walked the earth as a man, he forgave sins which only God can do. <u>This forgiving of sins pointed to Jesus' Deity</u>. Even His enemies knew that <u>only God can forgive sins</u> and <u>it is why they accused Him of blasphemy</u> as we read in **John 10:30-33:**

> "*30* **<u>I and my Father are one.</u>** *31* Then the Jews took up stones again to stone him. *32* Jesus answered them, Many good works have I shewed you from my Father; for which of those works do ye stone me? *33* **The Jews answered him, saying, For a good work we stone thee not; <u>but for blasphemy;</u> and <u>because that thou, being a man, makest thyself God.</u>**"

The question to be asked here would be, did Jesus Christ ever tell a lie? The answer would be No!

The Hebrew Israelites' Unbelief in the Deity of Jesus

The Hebrew Israelites do not believe in the Deity of Jesus Christ because they believe that worshiping Jesus Christ is idolatry. They accuse Christians of practicing idolatry. When I was a little boy growing up, the old folks would say, "The more the devil talks, the more he tells on himself."

This next point is for anyone in any religion that does not believe that God took on human flesh as Jesus because **everyone must believe that Jesus Christ came in the flesh** according to **1 John 4:3:**

> "<u>And every spirit that confesseth not that Jesus Christ is come in the flesh is not of God</u>:

and **this is that spirit of antichrist,** whereof ye have heard that it should come; and even now already is it in the world."

Know that every spirit that <u>confesses not</u> that Jesus Christ came in the flesh is not of God but is the spirit of antichrist. This is why **2 John verses 9-10** says that whosoever abided not in the doctrine of Christ hath not God.

> **"Whosoever transgresseth, and <u>abideth not in the doctrine of Christ</u>, hath not God.** He that abideth in the doctrine of Christ, he hath both the Father and the Son. *10* **If there come any unto you, and bring not this doctrine, receive him not into your house, <u>neither bid him God speed</u>."**

We cannot make anyone believe in the truth. The Spirit of God must be involved in order to reach someone with the truth of God's Word. Therefore, when someone comes to you with a false doctrine, as we see in the scripture above, **do not bid them goodbye!**

Many Preachers Do Not Believe in the Doctrine of the Trinity

Our God being **One God** and yet in **3 Distinct Persons,** is clearly revealed in scriptures. There are many preachers that do not believe in the doctrine of the Trinity even after reading the Bible. God reveals Himself as the One and Only God, yet **He <u>refers to Himself</u> in the Plural Form** as we see in **Genesis 1:26:**

> "God said let **<u>us</u>** make man in **<u>our</u>** image, in **<u>our</u>** likeness…"

The word **God** in the **Hebrew language** in this verse above, is **Elohim;** it is **plural.** Sometimes, the word refers to angels and men, but remember that the context here is that **God is referring to Himself in the Plural Form.**

We see it again in **Genesis 3:22** when **"God said the man is become as <u>one of us</u>."** Notice the language God uses in referring to Himself in the plural — **"<u>one of us</u>."** Jesus Christ is **One** of **those Persons** that God is talking with; God is Father, Son and Holy Spirit. To make it simple, I will put it like this: **The Father did not die on the Cross, the Holy Spirit did not die on the Cross but <u>the Son died on the Cross</u>.** We can also see Jesus Christ refer to Himself as **"The Almighty"** in **Revelation 1:8:**

> **"I am Alpha and Omega, the beginning and the ending,** saith the Lord, which **is,** and which **was,** and which **is to come, <u>the Almighty</u>."**

Jesus Christ also made a statement that revealed His Deity in **John 8:56-58.** He said to the Jews that Abraham rejoiced to see His day and that he (Abraham) saw it and was glad. The people responded by saying, **you are not even 50 years old, and have you seen Abraham?** Jesus responded by saying, 'Before Abraham was **<u>I am</u>**:"

> **"56 Your father Abraham rejoiced to see my day: and he saw it, and was glad.** 57 Then said the Jews unto him, **Thou art not yet fifty years old, and hast thou seen Abraham?** 58 Jesus said unto them, Verily, verily, I say unto you, **<u>Before Abraham was, I am</u>."**

The God of the Hebrews is known as the **I Am** that sent Moses into Egypt **so the Jews knew very well what the Lord Jesus had just said** to them; **they heard it loud and clear!** The question is, **when did Abraham see Jesus?** For the answer, you would have to go back to **Genesis Chapter 18.**

The Theophany of Jesus Christ

When you read **Genesis Chapter 18**, it gives us an account of the **3 Visitors** that came into the Abraham's camp. I want you to notice in the excerpt of the scriptures below that **the One that did all the talking was Jesus Christ!** Abraham made food for the Lord Jesus and the Lord Jesus gave Sarah a son. Abraham also saw the Lord destroy of Sodom. We see **their encounter** in **Genesis 18:1-21:**

"1**And the LORD appeared unto him (Abraham) in the plains of Mamre:** and he sat in the tent door in the heat of the day; 2 **And he lift up his eyes and looked, and, lo, three men stood by him:** and when he saw them, he ran to meet them from the tent door, and **bowed himself toward the ground,** 3 **And said, My Lord, if now I have found favour in thy sight, pass not away, I pray thee, from thy servant:** 4 Let a little water, I pray you, be fetched, and wash your feet, and rest yourselves under the tree: 5 And I will fetch a morsel of bread, and comfort ye your hearts; after that ye shall pass on: for therefore are ye come to your servant. And they said, So do, as thou hast said…

7 And Abraham ran unto the herd, and fetcht a calf tender and good, and gave it unto a young man; and he hasted to dress it. 8 **And he**

took butter, and milk, and the calf which he had dressed, and set it before them; and he stood by them under the tree, and they did eat. *9* And they said unto him, **Where is Sarah thy wife?** And he said, Behold, in the tent. *10* And he (the Lord) said, **I will certainly return unto thee according to the time of life; and, lo, Sarah thy wife shall have a son.** And Sarah heard it in the tent door, which was behind him.

11 Now Abraham and Sarah were old and well stricken in age; and it ceased to be with Sarah after the manner of women. *12* Therefore Sarah laughed within herself, saying, After I am waxed old shall I have pleasure, my lord being old also? *13* **And the LORD said unto Abraham, Wherefore did Sarah laugh, saying, Shall I of a surety bear a child, which am old? *14* Is anything too hard for the LORD? At the time appointed I will return unto thee, according to the time of life, and Sarah shall have a son.**

15 Then Sarah denied, saying, I laughed not; for she was afraid. And he said, Nay; but thou didst laugh. *16* And **the men rose up from thence, and looked toward Sodom:** and Abraham went with them to bring them on the way. *17* **And the LORD said, Shall I hide from Abraham that thing which I do**... *20* **And the LORD said,** Because the cry of Sodom and Gomorrah is great, and because their sin is very grievous; *21* I will go down now, and see whether they have done altogether according to the cry of it, which is come unto me; and if not, I will know."

This is what is called a 'Theophany.' **A Theophany is a <u>Visible Appearance of God</u> to a human. Jesus Christ is the only <u>physically visible Person</u> in the Godhead** (Colossians 1:15). <u>**There were several appearances of Jesus in the Old Testament**</u>; yes, appearances of Jesus Christ. He is truly worthy of our Praise and Worship.

God the Father Called Jesus Christ God

I want you to know that **God the Father** called Jesus Christ **God** in **Hebrews 1:8-9**:

> "But unto the **Son <u>he</u>** (God the Father) saith, <u>**Thy throne, O God, is for ever and ever**</u>: a sceptre of righteousness is the sceptre of thy kingdom. *9* **Thou hast loved righteousness, and hated iniquity; therefore God, even thy God, hath anointed thee with the oil of gladness above thy fellows.**"

Furthermore, **God the Father has commanded every knee to bow at the name of Jesus and every tongue to confess that Jesus Christ is Lord to God's glory** as we see in **Philippians 2:9-11**:

> "*9* Wherefore God also hath highly exalted him (Jesus), and given him a name which is above every name: *10* **That at the name of Jesus <u>every knee should bow</u>, of things in heaven, and things in earth, and things under the earth;** *11* And <u>**that every tongue should confess that Jesus Christ is Lord**</u>, **to the glory of God the Father.**"

You see, Jesus Christ is more than a mere man; He is a 100% Man and 100% God at the same time. He is the **Theos-Anthropos** or the **God-man. He had to be a God-man in order to reconcile man back to God within Himself.** He is the <u>Only Way</u> that man can get back to God.

No Hope of Salvation for the Hebrew Israelites

Again, **the danger in the message of the Hebrew Israelites is that they deny the Deity Jesus Christ.** As a result, **there is no real hope of Salvation for them because without Jesus Christ, there is no Salvation;** they have no viable way to God aside of Jesus. They are fulfilling what the Apostle Paul said, **forever learning but are unable to come into the knowledge of the truth.** They are unable to **acknowledge** the truth.

A Word about Christology

Christology is the part of theology that is concerned with the nature and work of Jesus Christ. The Hebrew Israelites are in fact, antichrists because they deny the Deity of Jesus Christ! They are very religious but lost. There is a very simple answer to the question: **Who Is Jesus Christ? <u>Jesus Christ is God</u> and He is worthy of all of our Worship and Praise. Jesus Christ is <u>One of the Persons in the Triune God</u>;** He was with God in the beginning.

the Theo-anthropos or the God-man: he had to be
a God-man in order to reconcile man self to God
which Himself, He is the Only W
Him to man.

Chapter 9
The Christians' Defense against Satan's Lies

Importance of Praying and Studying the Word of God

The Christian's defense against satan's lies is **living in obedience to the Word of God.** Another defense against satan's lies is being **rooted and grounded in the knowledge of our Lord and Savior Jesus Christ.** This is accomplished through a **strong prayer life and intensive study of God's Word** (the Bible). Also, with **strong fellowship with the Holy Spirit,** the mature Christians **can hold others accountable when it comes to sound doctrines.** The Holy Spirit is God's helper sent to enable us to live in obedience to God's Word and to convict us when we sin. We Christians are not perfect but are forgiven of all our trespasses against God and given a clear conscience to be confident toward God; **we stand by Grace.**

The Battleground of Spiritual Warfare

The Christian life is a battleground of spiritual warfare and it involves a constant struggle with the forces of darkness until the day we fall asleep (die). This is why we are commanded in **Ephesians 6:10-18** to put on the whole armor of God that we may be able to stand against all strategies of the devil:

> "10 Finally, my brethren, be strong in the Lord, and in the power of his might. 11 **Put on the whole armour of God, that ye may be able to stand against the wiles of the devil.** 12 **For**

we wrestle not against flesh and blood, but against principalities, against powers, against the rulers of the darkness of this world, against spiritual wickedness in high places. 13 Wherefore <u>take unto you the whole armour of God, that ye may be able to withstand in the evil day, and having done all, to stand.</u>

14 Stand therefore, having **your loins girt about with truth, and having on the breastplate of righteousness;** 15 And **your feet shod with the preparation of the gospel of peace;** 16 Above all, **taking the shield of faith, wherewith ye shall be able to quench all the fiery darts of the wicked.** 17 And **take the helmet of salvation, and <u>the sword of the Spirit, which is the word of God</u>:** 18 **Praying always with all prayer and supplication in the Spirit,** and watching thereunto with all perseverance and supplication for all saints."

Fighting against false doctrines is spiritual warfare because, the Bible says that **there are doctrines of demons** as we see **1 Timothy 4:1-2:**

"Now the Spirit speaketh expressly, that in the latter times some shall depart from the faith, giving heed to seducing spirits, and doctrines of devils; 2 Speaking lies in hypocrisy; having their conscience seared with a hot iron."

Christians Should Study Church History

Church History is another subject that should be studied by all Christians. When you do, you will learn about the past **heretical** and **erroneous** teachings that the **Church dealt** with along with the **persecutions of the early Christians.** Also, you will learn about how many of them were martyred. There is a saying that, **"The truth is not new; if it is new, it is not true."** **Many claim to be getting new revelation knowledge from God but there is <u>one problem</u> with that claim because the Lord Jesus Christ is God's last revelation to man.** Now, there is a thing called illumination but it works in accordance with God's Word (the Bible) and by His Spirit.

Study the Customs and Cultures of People in the Bible

Another subject to research would be, the Customs and Cultures of the People in the Bible. Doing this will help with your study of the Bible so that you are grounded in what is written in it. To me, there is nothing worse than an ignorant preacher that whenever he opens his mouth, he reveals himself as clueless of what he is talking about. Again, sound expository preaching and teaching is the best kind of preaching and teaching to edify the body of Christ (the Church). Meaning, "thus saith the Lord God" kind of preaching and teaching. This type of preaching that is lacking in the Church today.

The Miseducation of Preachers

The 'modern Church' has been infiltrated with all kinds of erroneous teachings because a lot of pastors have been miseducated and led astray. This is because many of them did not first take the time to thoroughly study the Bible. If they had, they probably would have had some discernment when it comes to the things of God written in the Bible. **The good news is that God always has a remnant that are loyal and faithful to Him no matter how bad it seems to get.** We can be confident that God's truth will never be defeated by satan's lies.

The individual Christian is responsible for his or her personal study of God's Word as this is where one's discernment develops. Since the beginning of the Church, there has been deceptions but right now, deception is at an all-time high. The Lord Jesus knew that this would happen and it is why He said in **Matthew 24:4**, "Do not let anyone mislead you." **Right now, there are a lot of popular preachers that are not rooted and grounded in God's Word and as a result, they are leading many away from God's truth.**

The Bible has a lot to say about the **end-time deception** that will culminate in the rise of the Antichrist. Meaning, the one-world leader that is **mentioned in the Book of Revelation and who will lead a one-world government and economy. The Lord Jesus Christ is victorious in the end along with His people. Afterwards, Jesus Christ will set up His Kingdom on the earth for 1,000 years.** At the end, there will be a **New Heaven** and a **New Earth.** This is the Christian's hope for the future. God promised it and He is faithful to keep His Word.

The Test of a True Prophet and a False Prophet
One third of the Bible is prophetic, which means that **God's signature** is on it and only He knows the future. **The test to find out if someone is prophesying on behalf of what God said, is that what he said must come to pass; no exceptions and no room for error.**

We see this in **Deuteronomy 18:21-22** scriptures on how to test for a true prophet and a false prophet:

> "*21* **And if thou say in thine heart, How shall we know the word which the LORD hath not spoken?** *22* **When a prophet speaketh in the name of the LORD, if the thing follow not, nor come to pass, that is the thing which the LORD hath not spoken,** but the prophet hath spoken it presumptuously: **thou shalt not be afraid of him.**"

Chapter 10
Why Did God Give the Law?

God's Law reveals His righteous standard of perfection so, in order for someone to be declared righteous before Him, the person has to meet God's righteous standard. Also, God's Law reveals God's holiness and the sinfulness of man. For example, if someone could live to be 1,000,000 years old and **only sin once,** he would be guilty of breaking the Law which is punishable by death — **Romans 6:23:**

> "**For the wages of sin is death;** but **the gift of God is eternal life through Jesus Christ our Lord.**"

Jesus Christ took it a step further when He made God's righteous standard a matter of the heart by saying, "**If a man looks at a woman and lusts after her in his heart, he has committed adultery with her already in his heart**" (Matthew 5:28). There is no exception to this 'whosoever.' This is God's requirement in order to be declared righteous before Him which is impossible for us to do. The Bible says in **Romans 3:20** that by the works of the Law, no man will be justified:

> "Therefore **by the deeds of the law there shall no flesh be justified in his sight**: for by the law is the knowledge of sin."

And also in **Galatians 2:16:**

> "**Knowing that a man is not justified by the works of the law, but by the faith of Jesus Christ,** even we have believed in Jesus Christ, that we might be justified by the faith of Christ,

and not by the works of the law: **for by the works of the law shall no flesh be justified."**

God did not give us the Law to keep but, the Hebrew Israelites teach that keeping the Law is the way to obtain Salvation. The truth is that **the Law was given to us to show us our sinfulness and for us to know that we need to believe the Gospel of Jesus Chris for our justification by faith.** The message of the Hebrew Israelites is dangerous with no hope beyond death.

Salvation Through Physical Genealogy?

The Hebrew Israelites believe that their physical identity or genealogy goes back to the Hebrews of the Bible making them special as God's chosen people. The Apostle Paul dealt with this type of thinking in **Romans 2:14-29**:

> "*14* **For when the Gentiles, which have not the law, do by nature the things contained in the law, these, having not the law, are a law unto themselves:** *15* **Which shew the work of the law written in their hearts, their conscience also bearing witness, and their thoughts the mean while accusing or else excusing one another;)** *16* In the day when God shall judge the secrets of men by Jesus Christ according to my gospel. *17* **Behold, thou art called a Jew, and restest in the law, and makest thy boast of God**...
>
> *26* Therefore if the uncircumcision keep the righteousness of the law, shall not his uncircumcision be counted for circumcision? *27* **And shall not uncircumcision which is**

by nature, if it fulfil the law, judge thee, who by the letter and circumcision dost transgress the law? 28 For <u>he is not a Jew, which is one outwardly;</u> neither is that circumcision, which is outward in the flesh: 29 But <u>he is a Jew, which is one inwardly; and circumcision is that of the heart, in the spirit, and not in the letter;</u> whose praise is not of men, but of God."

As you can see above, the scriptures teach that a man is not justified based on just being a Jew in the physical; <u>a Jew is justified by faith in Jesus Christ</u>. According to Paul's writing which is inspired by the Holy Spirit, if the **uncircumcision** (Gentiles) meet the requirements of the Law by having faith in Jesus Christ, they would be accepted by God unlike the Jews with no faith. Meaning that, a Jew without faith in Christ would not be accepted by God. Again, the early Church dealt with this false teaching and they called the ones advocating it '**Judaizers.**' According to **2 Timothy 3:16**, the Word of God in the Bible is to be used to correct erroneous teachings:

"<u>All scripture is given by inspiration of God,</u> and is profitable for doctrine, for <u>reproof,</u> for <u>correction,</u> for <u>instruction in righteousness</u>."

Many who teach incorrect doctrines frown upon this text of scripture because they do not want anyone to question them about what they are teaching. A true biblical teacher or preacher welcomes questions concerning what they are teaching. **The sign of a cult is that the leader is a dictator.**

The New Testament was Mentioned in the Old Testament

The New Covenant was mentioned in **Jeremiah 31:33** where God says:

> "But this shall be the covenant that I will make with the house of Israel; After those days, saith the Lord, I will put my law in their inward parts, and write it in their hearts; and will be their God, and they shall be my people."

According to **Hebrews 10:16**, this New Covenant was fulfilled and made possible by Jesus Christ. The mistake the Hebrew Israelites make with the above prophecy is that they only relate it to themselves. They forget about **Ephesians 3:1-6** where the Apostle Paul said that the Mystery about Christ and His Church was not made known in past ages, but now is made known. This is the Mystery **"that the Gentiles should be fellow heirs, and of the same body, and partakers of his promise in Christ by the gospel."** Meaning that, God has chosen the Jews and the Gentiles who put their faith and trust in Jesus Christ as His people! **This is the body of believers that is called the <u>Church</u> or the <u>Body of Christ</u>.**

The Law was given by God to bring us to Christ for Salvation by faith. The Gospel of Jesus Christ is simple. **We are saved by grace through faith in Christ Jesus alone. Therefore, if anyone adds or takes away from this truth, then it is not the Gospel Jesus Christ.** The Hebrew Israelites are guilty of not understanding the Gospel of Jesus Christ; they interpret the Bible by ignoring scriptures. You cannot ignore scriptures or make the Bible seem to contradict itself.

The challenge that I would like to put out to everyone here is, learn to study the Word of God accurately and keep everything in context; meaning, no contradiction. We must also develop **a strong prayer life** and **depend on God to lead us** in this spiritual warfare we are in. Familiarize yourself with what it means to "put on the whole Armor of God" as mentioned in Ephesians 6:10-18. In the battle that we are in right now, we cannot be lazy Christians. You must also be encouraged and remember that Jesus said that **He would not leave us or forsake us** (Hebrews 13:5).

The Bereans (Believers at Berea) that are recorded in Acts chapter 17 are noted as good examples for us to imitate. They searched the scriptures daily to see if the Apostle Paul was in fact, telling the truth. There are many preachers; I mean, not a few preachers who preach and teach things contrary to the Bible in the name of Jesus Christ. For you to know this, you will have to familiarize yourself with the Word of God and rightly divide it. In other words, you will have to study to know the truth written in the Bible.

There is a saying, **"You can lead a man to knowledge, but you cannot make him think."** Some professing Christians believe that you do not have to study the Word of God and that all you need is the Holy Spirit. Do not get me wrong, you do need the Holy Spirit but you still need to study God's Word (the Bible). The Holy Spirit will use God's Word to help you in your walk with the Lord. It is only then that you will be able to recognize those who are teaching sound doctrines.

The preaching of the Cross is foolishness to those who perish (1 Corinthians 1:18). A dear brother I knew who was a pastor but who is now with the Lord (Dr. Ben Wilkinson), told me this and I agreed with him, **"The preaching of the Gospel of Jesus Christ serves a purpose to the hearers. It will either <u>draw them to Salvation</u> or they will be <u>more damned than before they heard it.</u>"** Jesus Christ is the 'Divider' of men; either you believe in Him, or you do not. Where you will spend Eternity depends on those two decisions.

God has a testimony concerning Himself that is greater than anything anyone else has to say about Him. We read this in **1 John 5:7-9:**

> **"7 For there are three that bear record in heaven, the Father, the Word, and the Holy Ghost**: and **these three are one**. 8 And there are three that bear witness in earth, the Spirit, and the water, and the blood: and these three agree in one. 9 **If we receive the witness of men, the witness of God is greater: for this is the witness of God which he hath testified of his Son."**

About the Wisdom of God

The Apostle Paul wrote about this Wisdom in **1 Corinthians 2:1-16** (NKJ):

> **"1When I first came to you, dear brothers and sisters, I didn't use lofty words and impressive wisdom to tell you God's secret plan.** 2 For decided that while I was with you, I forget everything except Jesus Christ, the one who was crucified. 3 I came to you in weakness-timid and trembling. 4 And my message and my preaching were very plain. Rather

than using clever and persuasive speeches, I relied only on the power of the Holy Spirit. *5* **I did this so you would trust not in human wisdom but in the power of God.** *6* Yet when I am among mature believers, I do speak with words of wisdom, but not the kind of wisdom that belongs to this world or to the rulers of this world, who are soon forgotten.

7 **No, the wisdom we speak of is the mystery of God — his plan that was previously hidden, even though he made it for our ultimate glory before the world began.** *8* But the rulers of this world have not understood it, if they had, they would not have crucified our glorious Lord. *9* That is what the scriptures mean when they say, No eye has seen, or ear has heard, And no mind has imagined. What God has prepared? For those who love him. *10* **But it was to us that God revealed these things by his Spirit. For his Spirit searches out everything and shows us God's deep secrets.** *11* No one can know a person's thoughts except that person's own spirit, and **no one can know God's thoughts except God's own Spirit.**

12 **And we have received God's Spirit (not the world's spirit), so we can know the wonderful things God has freely given us.** *13* When we tell you these things, we do not use words that come from human wisdom. **Instead, we speak words given to us by the Spirit, using the Spirit's words to explain spiritual truths.** *14* But people who aren't spiritual can't receive these truths from God's Spirit. It all sounds foolish to them, and **they can't receive it, for**

only those who are spiritual can understand what the Spirit means. *15* **Those who spiritual can evaluate all things,** but they themselves cannot be evaluated by others. *16* For, Who can know the Lord's thoughts? Who knows enough to teach him? **But we understand these things, for we have the mind of Christ.**"

These scriptures above explain what we are dealing with when it comes to sharing God's truth with others. The Lord Jesus said it best in **John 10:26-28** where He said:

"*26* **But ye believe not, because ye are not of my sheep,** as I said unto you. *27* **My sheep hear my voice, and I know them, and they follow me**: *28* And I give unto them eternal life; and they shall never perish, neither shall any man pluck them out of my hand."

Chapter 11
Who Are the Gentiles?

The Definition of a Gentile

The Hebrew Israelites do not adhere to biblical and traditional definitions of words. For example, the word **Gentile**. A <u>Gentile</u> is defined as **a person who is not a Jew or a Hebrew; meaning, <u>someone who is not</u> of the lineage of the 12 Tribes of Israel. These Tribes are from the 12 sons of Jacob. This is the Jacob whose name was later changed by God to Israel.** Some Hebrew Israelites say that 10 of the 12 Tribes (the Northern Kingdom part of Israel), eventually became Gentiles. They say this in order to support their erroneous teaching of **'Israel only doctrine.'** **This doctrine teaches that 'Israel only' (them) will be saved.** They reject the scriptures which teach that **God has <u>extended His Grace</u> to the Gentiles for Salvation** — Titus 2:11:

> "For the **<u>grace of God</u>** that **bringeth salvation** hath **<u>appeared to all men</u>**."

And also in **Ephesians 3:1-6:**

> "*1* For this cause I Paul, the prisoner of Jesus Christ for you Gentiles, *2* If ye have heard of the dispensation of the grace of God which is given me to you-ward: *3* How that by revelation he made known unto me the mystery; (as I wrote afore in few words, *4* **Whereby, when ye read, ye may understand my knowledge in the <u>mystery of Christ</u>)** *5* Which in other ages was not made known unto the sons of men, as it

is now revealed unto his holy apostles and prophets by the Spirit; 6 **That the Gentiles should be fellowheirs, and of the same body, and partakers of his promise in Christ by the gospel.**"

It is repeated in Galatians 3:8, Acts chapters 10 and 15. To be clear about this, the Apostle Paul addressed Gentiles; meaning those who were **born as Gentiles** as we read in **Ephesians 2:11-13:**

> "11 **Wherefore remember, that <u>ye being in time past Gentiles in the flesh</u>, who are called Uncircumcision by that which is called the Circumcision in the flesh made by hands;** 12 That at that time **ye were without Christ, being aliens from the commonwealth of Israel, and strangers from the covenants of promise, having no hope, and without God in the world:** 13 But <u>**now in Christ Jesus ye who sometimes were far off are made nigh by the blood of Christ**</u>."

Contrary to this biblical truth, some Hebrew Israelites teach that Gentiles cannot be saved. **Be assured that <u>there is not one text of scripture reference</u> where a <u>Hebrew</u> became a <u>Gentile</u>.** Therefore, the 'Israel only doctrine' is false because God has extended His Grace to both Jews and Gentiles for Salvation.

Examples of Gentiles Saved by Grace in the Old Testament

There are examples in the Old Testament of Gentiles being saved by God's Grace through faith such as **Rahab** the harlot who is mentioned in Hebrews 11.

There is also **Ruth;** a Moabite mentioned in the Book of Ruth. The Hebrew Israelites make a 'play on words,' in their **'Israel only doctrine.'**

The Fallacy of Changing the Word Gentile to Mean Hebrew

Another example of the Hebrew Israelites' doctrinal error is in the use of the words **Gentile** and **Heathen.** Biblically, these two words are used **interchangeably** because **they mean the same thing** but, the Hebrew Israelites have come up with their definition of these words. **They have changed the word <u>Gentiles</u> to mean <u>Hebrews</u> of the Northern Kingdom of Israel.** I have already stated that there is no scripture reference where a Hebrew became a Gentile.

In their deception, the Hebrew Israelites refer to the Hebrews of the Northern Kingdom as Gentiles and everyone else as Heathens. **We know from scriptures that Gentiles and Heathens mean the same thing—** all non-Jewish people or the people who are not the descendants of Abraham. **Abraham was called the Hebrew in Genesis 14:13 hence his descendants are called Hebrews.** No Gentile is a Hebrew because **being Hebrew is by natural birth through Abraham.**

> "And there came one that had escaped, **and told Abram the Hebrew;** for he dwelt in the plain of Mamre the Amorite, brother of Eshcol, and brother of Aner: and these were confederate with Abram."

Again, the Hebrew Israelites teach that the heathens cannot be saved by God but we are told in Galatians 3:8 that **God will justify the heathen through faith.**

Also, Romans 3:4 says, "Let God be true and every man a liar." This is why as Christians, we must study God's Word in order to refute the false teachers who change the definition of words and pull scriptures out of context in their attempts to support their false narratives and erroneous teachings.

The reason why the Hebrew Israelites are wrong about scriptures is because they do not have a true understanding of the Gospel of Jesus Christ. They do not know who Jesus Christ really is because they do not have the Holy Spirit to "lead and guide them in all truth" as the Word of God says.

I reiterate, please, study Church History and know all the 66 Books of the Bible in depth for your own protection from deceptions.

Chapter 12
The Heart of the Gospel of Jesus Christ

Christianity is the only Faith on earth which teaches that Salvation is by Grace through faith in Jesus Christ alone. All other Faiths teach that salvation is earned through works. In other words, they believe that salvation is earned through good works. In line with these other Faiths, the Hebrew Israelites teach that salvation is earned by keeping the Law; meaning, the Law God gave to Moses. The Bible teaches in Romans 3:20 and in Galatians 2:16 that by the works of the Law shall no one will be justified before God. A lot of Hebrew Israelites reject the New Testament all together; yes, they reject Jesus Christ! The truth is that without Jesus Christ, there is no Salvation. Let us look at how God provided Salvation through Jesus Christ.

The First Prophecy about Jesus Christ
The first prophecy concerning Jesus Christ is **Genesis 3:15, the Seed of the woman** will crush the head of serpent. Meaning that the offspring of the woman will have the power to destroy the works of the devil and it was also pointing to the Deity of this offspring:

> "And **I will put enmity between thee and the woman, and between thy seed and her seed; <u>it shall bruise thy head</u>, and thou shalt bruise his heel."**

Jesus Christ was born of a virgin and He came from Heaven to become a Man. Only God has the power to destroy the works of the devil. The offspring of the woman would be God and Man at the same time.

We All Died in Adam but
Made Alive in Christ

God gave the Law to Moses and according to the Law, for a man to be justified, he must live up to the standards of the Law without ever committing an act of sin one time! The problem with this is that all mankind was born in Adam; meaning that **we are all born sinners.**

As written in **1 Corinthians 15:22**, in Adam, we all died because of our sins.

> **"For as in Adam all die, <u>even so in Christ shall all be made alive</u>."**

Also, we are told in **Romans 6:23** that the wage of sin is death. **The problem that God has with man is sin; sin separates us from God spiritually**. This spiritual separation is called 'spiritual death.' God's plan to redeem man back to Himself was for Jesus Christ to be born under the Law and to meet all the righteous requirements of Law. Meaning that, **Jesus would be the only Man to live under the Law without breaking the Law even one time; He lived a perfect and sinless life.** This pleased God and He then placed all the sins of mankind on Christ. This includes all humanity's sins going all the way back to Adam and Eve. God placed them all on Jesus Christ on the Cross:

> **"For the wages of sin is death; but <u>the gift of God is eternal life through Jesus Christ our Lord</u>."**

The Misconception of the Hebrew Israelites Concerning Justification

When an individual comes to Christ in faith, their sins are forgiven and God imputes Christ righteousness to that individual's account. The Resurrection of Jesus Christ made that individual to be justified. **Jesus Christ is man's only hope of Salvation and of being delivered from the power of sin.** Once an individual is justified by faith in Jesus Christ, **God then sees the person as though he had never sinned.** Paul's Epistle to the Romans goes into detail concerning "Justification by Faith."

The Hebrew Israelites have a misconception concerning justification by faith. They have the idea that Christians are teaching that we do not have to keep the Law and that we are therefore, sinning against the Law. In fact, our faith in Jesus Christ fulfills the Law. The Law was given to bring us to Christ and that we might be justified by faith as we see in **Galatians 3:22-25:**

"22 But the scripture hath concluded all under sin, that the promise by faith of Jesus Christ might be given to them that believe. 23 **But before faith came, we were** kept **under the law,** shut up unto the faith which should afterwards be revealed. 24 Wherefore **the law was our schoolmaster to bring us unto Christ, that we might be justified by faith**. 25 **But after that faith is come,** we are no longer under a schoolmaster."

Their Misunderstanding of 'Sinless' in the Old Testament

Another misunderstanding displayed by the Hebrew Israelites involves the use of words such as **'sinless,' 'blameless'** and **'perfect'** in the Old Testament. They think because God used these words to describe individuals such as **Noah, Enoch, Abraham, Job,** etc., that it means that these individuals were sinless. The definition of these words gives the truth of what is meant by the use of the words. **For example, the words 'perfect' and 'blameless' mean that God has justified an individual by faith. It means that the individual has their sins forgiven and has been declared righteous by God.** The individual cannot be accused of sin before God because he has been acquitted of all sins. The Book Romans go into detail about being justified by faith before God. Take a look at **Romans 5:1-2:**

> **"Therefore being justified by faith, we have peace with God through our Lord Jesus Christ:** 2 By whom also we have access by faith into this grace wherein we stand, and rejoice in hope of the glory of God."

No More Condemnation in Christ

In the New Covenant, the believers in Christ are acquitted of all sins; past, present and future. This is what the Apostle Paul meant in **Colossians 2:14** when he was talking about what Christ did for us on the Cross:

> **"Blotting out the handwriting of ordinances that was against us,** which was **contrary to us,** and <u>**took it of the way, nailing it to his cross**</u>."

He concluded by stating the following in **Romans 8:1:**

> "There is therefore <u>now no condemnation to them which are in Christ Jesus</u> who walk not after the flesh, <u>but after the Spirit</u>."

The Hebrew Israelites are trying to please God in the flesh by keeping the Law; something that is impossible to do. Therefore, the 'gospel' they advocate is no Gospel at all. **The word Gospel means "Good News" that comes from God Himself.** The Hebrew Israelites have no good news from God and at the end of their lives, the Law that they are trying to keep will condemn them. **Unless the Hebrew Israelites repent, receive the Good News from God and believe on the Lord Jesus Christ for their Salvation, they will be lost for all eternity.** What a sad conclusion for 'Salvation by Works' message which presents itself as truth but is nothing but a counterfeit from the enemy of our souls.

The Hebrew Israelites Need to Receive God's Love in Christ

In conclusion, I say that the Hebrew Israelites are some of the most unloving people because they show no evidence of having the Spirit of God. Therefore, they do not manifest the **Fruit of the Spirit** that are outlined in **Galatians 5:22-23**. They are self-righteous and self-righteous people are fault finders who condemn others:

> "But the <u>fruit of the Spirit</u> is love, joy, peace, longsuffering, gentleness, goodness, faith, 23 Meekness, temperance: <u>against such there is no law</u>."

They need Christ so they can receive God's Agape (unconditional) love.

For those who want to make Jesus Christ their Lord, below is a prayer of Salvation to help you do just that:

Prayer of Salvation

"Heavenly Father, after reading this book, I now know that my beliefs as a Hebrew Israelite are wrong not pleasing to You. I also realize now that these wrong beliefs will not lead me to You. Therefore, I repent today and ask for Your forgiveness for all my previous wrong beliefs. I now believe that Jesus Christ is Your Son and that He came into this world in the flesh as a man. He died for my sins on the Cross and was buried but on the third day, You raised Him from the dead.

Today, Lord Jesus Christ, I repent of my sins, forgive me my sins, wash me with Your Blood and be my Lord. Please give me Eternal Life and baptize me with the Holy Spirit to help me know the Truth of Your Word and guide me all the days of my life. Thank You for hearing me and saving my soul."

About the Author

Carlton Green is from Atlanta, Georgia and he graduated from Charles Lincoln Harper High School. He served in the United States' Marine Corps from 1977 to 1981; he spent most of his tour of duty at Camp David, Maryland from 1978 to 1981. **Carlton became a Christian in August 1978 while he was in the Marine Corps and he started studying Eschatology out of curiosity.** Later, he began a serious **'Inductive Bible Study'** of the entire Bible from October 1982.

In 2001, he launched a Radio Show entitled, **The Bread of Life Broadcast** and about a year later, he changed the platform to a **Call-in Talk Show** called, **The Berean Investigative Research Broadcast.**

He also started a Bible Study in 2002 for the purpose of encouraging Christians to correctly study the Bible. He has produced several Seminars dealing with subjects such as **Christian Apologetics, Freemasonry, The Word of Faith Prosperity Gospel, The Jehovah Witnesses, Islam, The Doctrine of The Trinity and Church History**.